TEST YOUR INTELLIGENCE

TEST YOUR INTELLIGENCE

By Norman Sullivan

BLANDFORD

First published in the UK 1988 by Blandford Press
an imprint of Cassell plc.
Villiers House, 41/47 Strand, London WC2N 5JE
Reprinted 1988
Reprinted 1989
Reprinted 1990 (twice)
Reprinted 1991
Reprinted 1992

Distributed in the United States by
Sterling Publishing Co., Inc.,
387 Park Avenue South, New York, NY 10016

Distributed in Australia by
Capricorn Link (Australia) Pty Ltd.,
PO Box 665, Lane Cove, NSW 2066

British Library Cataloguing in Publication Data

Sullivan, Norman
  Test your Intelligence.
  Vol. 1
  1. intelligence tests
  I. Title
  153.9'3   BF431

ISBN 0 7137 20115

Typeset by St. George Typesetting, Redruth, Cornwall
Printed in Great Britain by Cox & Wyman Ltd., Reading

CONTENTS

INTRODUCTION

If it is agreed that it is essential to exercise the brain as well as the body, then this book should provide mental therapy in plenty.

I do not claim that it will enable you to put a definitive rating on your IQ – indeed, what book *could*, in view of the many unknown elements involved, such as mental and chronological age? It will, however, enable you to make an assessment – albeit arbitrarily – of your aptitude for various subjects.

'Aptitude' might be defined as a natural propensity for a given subject; an inherent ability that allows one to excel, or at least do well, in a subject for which one has a natural flair. One who has a natural talent for performing mechanical skills might show no aptitude at all for artistic achievements or skills requiring verbal or numerical ability.

Practically everyone has a natural aptitude for something or other, and one person's flair is another person's bugbear. Children at school soon demonstrate in which direction their aptitude lies. One child shows an aptitude for history, but is hopeless at mathematics; one seems naturally gifted at music, but remains backward in English.

Aptitude, then, is an innate predilection for a certain subject or subjects, though it may allow ignorance of other subjects.

'Intelligence' is much wider in its implications and might be defined as 'the ability to reason quickly and logically in a subject, even though there is no natural aptitude for that subject; to be able to get to the root of a problem and from that arrive rationally, quickly and correctly at the solution.'

An aptitude test can evaluate a person's ability in a given

field with a reasonable expectancy of a valid assessment, and is often used by employers who have to judge the potential of a candidate for a position demanding specific qualities. If an employer wanted to select a suitable worker in a job that called for colour discrimination, he would hardly wish to employ one who was colour-blind. It is reasonable to suppose that he would devise a test to prove or disprove the colour awareness of the applicant. If a job entailed quick sorting, filing, or arranging items in a definite order, either alphabetically or otherwise, a test could be devised to highlight those qualities.

The tests in this book are designed to indicate the reader's individual aptitudes and are graded according to difficulty.

The main subjects dealt with are:

a) Verbal skills, knowledge of words, spelling and general knowledge;

b) Spatial discrimination and recognition of shapes, especially when the shapes change their position in relation to the viewer;

c) Numerical skills and recognition of sequences;

d) Logical reasoning and deduction on any subject.

Each test comprises a fairly equal mix of all these subjects, and they are arranged in three groups:

a) Easy

b) More difficult

c) Difficult.

A time limit has been imposed for each test, and it is important that you only record points scored within that time limit. If you have not completed the test within the time limit, you should carry on to the end of that test, but do not include any points scored in your official record. Instinctive appraisal may be more rewarding than prolonged consideration, so do not waste too much time pondering over any one problem; pass straight on to the next question. You can always go back to a problem that has stumped you if there is time in hand at the end of the test.

Remember, however, that accuracy is more important than speed, so try to aim for a compromise between dwelling too long on a problem you cannot answer quickly and passing to the next one without devoting a little time to the former. What appears to be obscure at first sight may become obvious when you return to it later and find that it triggers off an idea that previously eluded you.

Before commencing each test take a note of the time, and stop as soon as the time limit is reached (unless you have completed the test before then). As already mentioned, do not record any scores after the time limit is reached.

At the end of each test check your answers from the following pages and keep a note of your scores throughout.

Make sure you have writing materials handy for these reasons:

a) It is permissible to work out answers on paper, provided you do not use the paper for tracing purposes;

b) Some problems require an answer in words (as opposed to a letter or number);

c) You must retain a record of your scores until you have tackled all the tests.

After each **group** of tests you will be able to compare your score with the ratings given. Do not lose heart if you *appear* to have low scores for individual tests. My thanks go to the many people who have allowed themselves to be pre-tested, and from whom I have been able to establish comparative ratings and reasonable time limits.

As you will see when you reach the end of the book, where final ratings are shown, the averages recorded by these volunteers were extremely low. Whether this reflects on their low IQs or the high standard of the tests is open to question, but the important thing is that their ratings offer a basis from which you can make a comparison of your own results.

There   are   mixed   views   regarding   the   value   of

psychometrics as a means of assessing intelligence, but leaving aside any merits that these tests have in that context, they should certainly tax your cerebral capacity.

It may well be that you will prefer to go through the book without regard to time limits or ratings. The choice is yours, but in either event it should help you to pass the time in a pleasant and useful way.

It is my earnest hope that the problems will not only offer you food for thought, but a feast of mental entertainment and enjoyment – not to mention background experience for any tests of a similar nature that you may encounter at another time.

Now, pencil and paper at the ready? Timepiece handy? Then off you go. And no peeping at the answers in advance!

Good luck!

Norman Sullivan

GROUP I
EASY

TEST 1
(Time limit: 35 minutes)

1 What letter will complete this word?

2 Which one of these figures is wrong?

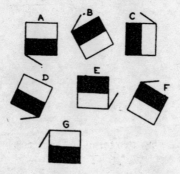

3 Add the two highest numbers and take away the sum of the three lowest numbers.

16 13 9 11 23 19
5 14 12 15 18 17

4 If 6 3 5 4 2 equals 5 2 6 3 4, what is: B C D E F ?

5   Join these syllables in pairs to make ten words:

REC	LET	LOON	WINK
AD	BAL	TOM	FUR
ER	ORD	BRE	TAB
ORE	CAT	HOOD	HER
BOY	SA	OUT	LE

6   Arrange these into four pairs:

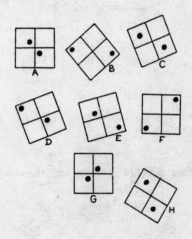

7   What are the last two terms in this series?
    Z   13   Y   14   W   16   T   19   –   –

8   Which is the odd one out?
  (A) LIRA
  (B) MARKS
  (C) DRACHMAE
  (D) RAND
  (E) FRANCS

15

9 Which is the odd one out?
   (A) Y L A P
   (B) A P R E O
   (C) V E E R U
   (D) R E N C O C T
   (E) S H E C S

10 Which of these is wrong?

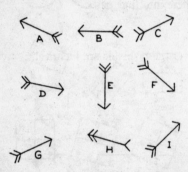

11 Which date does not conform with the others?
   (A) 1584   (D) 1809
   (B) 1692   (E) 1980
   (C) 1729

12 Which is the odd one out?
   (A) ELIGIBLE   (D) FOOLPROOF
   (B) SHEEPISH   (E) GNASHING
   (C) DELIGHTED

13 Arrange these words in alphabetical order:
   (A) ABRACADABRA   (E) ABACUS
   (B) ABOUT   (F) ABOULIA
   (C) ABBEY   (G) ABBOT
   (D) ABUNDANCE

14 Who has changed his expression?

15 Which two of these shields are identical?

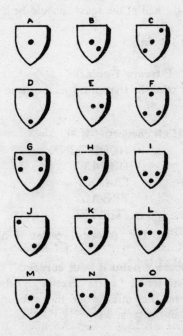

Now check your answers and keep a note of your score.

ANSWERS

1 **H (score 1 point).**
The word is ADHERE.

2 **A (score 1 point).**
When the diagonal line from the base-line of the square inclines to the right, as in C, E and G, the right half of the square is black.

When it inclines to the left, as in B, D and F, the bottom half of the square is black.

In A the right half of the square should be black.

3 17 **(score 1 point).**

4 D F B C E **(score 1 point).**
The letters must be transposed in the same order as the numbers.

5 **(Score 1 if all correct; $\frac{1}{2}$ if 8).**

REC-ORD	HOOD-WINK
CAT-ER	OUT-LET
TOM-BOY	SA-LOON
TAB-LE	BRE-AD
HER-BAL	FUR-ORE

6 AG BF CH DE **(score 1 point if all correct).**

7 P 23 **(score 1 point if both correct).**
Two separate series. Letters descend alphabetically, first to the next letter, then missing one, then two, and so on. The numbers rise in the same way.

8 (B) **(score 1 point).**
All the other currencies contain the letters RA in that order. In MARKS these letters are reversed.

9   (E) (score 1 point).
An anagram of CHESS. All the others are anagrams of
types of entertainment:
(A)   PLAY
(B)   OPERA
(C)   REVUE
(D)   CONCERT

10   H (score 1 point).
The point has two barbs instead of one, and one set of tail
feathers instead of two.

11   (C) (score 1 point).
The digits add to 19. In all the others they add to 18.

12   (B) (score 1 point).
It starts and ends with the same two letters. All the others
start and end with the same two letters reversed.

13   (E) (C) (G) (F) (B) (A) (D) (score 1 point).

14   J (score 1 point).
The mouth should be as in B and H.

15   B and M (score 1 point).

Remember to keep a note of your score.

NOTES

Although all the tests in this book are graded as to difficulty,
obviously in any one section some problems will be *relatively*
more difficult (or easier) than others.
    In drawing a distinction, the dividing line between a

difficult problem in one section and an easy one in the next is very slender, and the divisions are therefore notional.

However, in the final count this is immaterial, as the ultimate ratings are based on all the problems taken collectively.

In imposing time limits two factors have to be considered:

(1) The fact that some problems require fairly lengthy written answers (as opposed to simply writing a letter or a number);

(2) Some people write faster than others. Accordingly, these points have been taken into consideration, and where written answers are involved not only has a longer time limit been imposed, but the time has been taken from that of comparatively slow writers.

No 5 in the previous test took our volunteers longer – because of the amount of writing involved, and also because it called for a great deal of 'trial and error' deduction. Success depended largely on making a fortunate choice between alternatives.

Other problems which caused delay in answering – or failure to answer correctly – were 8 and 12, each calling for deductions beyond the obvious. In the case of 8, reasoning based on the fact that one currency is non-European would not be considered so outstandingly valid as the reason given in the answers.

TEST 2
(Time limit: 35 minutes)

1 What goes into the empty brackets?

144 (3625) 125
96 (1618) 126
112 (   ) 144

2 The words in the brackets must logically follow the previous word and precede the following word,
e.g. library (BOOK) token.

BULL
(   )
WATCH
(   )
BLOCK
(   )
STONE
(   )
PAPER
(   )
LETTER
(   )
OFFICE

3 Using your eye only, which is the missing brick?

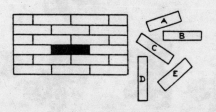

4 Which is the odd one out?

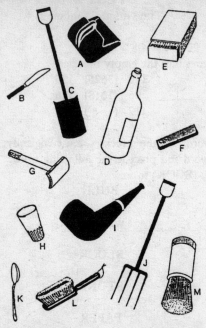

5 Arrange these strange-looking insects into four pairs.

6 What is X?

$$J - M - M - J - S - N - X$$

7 Which one is wrong?

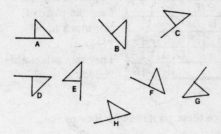

8 Arrange these labels into four pairs:

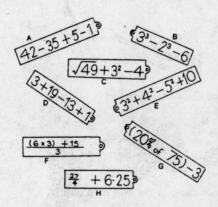

9 What is X?

10 Complete these words, for which definitions are given:

p	e	r						
	p	e	r					
		p	e	r				
			p	e	r			
				p	e	r		
					p	e	r	
						p	e	r

Staff
Surgical treatment
Take the place of
Not much hope!
Thrived
They take off clothes or paint!
Periodical

11 Arrange these patterns into four pairs.

12 Which of these is the odd man out?

4   18   16   8   24

13 Change RAIN into SNOW in three moves, changing TWO letters at a time.

```
    R A I N
  1 _ _ _ _
  2 _ _ _ _
  3 S N O W
```

24

14 Which is the odd one out?
   (A) PROVERBS   (D) CORINTHIANS
   (B) RUTH   (E) NUMBERS
   (C) EZEKIEL   (F) PSALMS

15 Assuming that the top two stars are correct, which of those below are wrong?

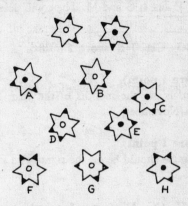

Now check your answers and keep a note of your score.

ANSWERS

1 1416 **(score 1 point).**

In the first example, divide the left-hand number by 4 and the right-hand number by 5.

In the second example, divide the left-hand number by 6 and the right-hand number by 7.

Therefore, in the third line, divide the left-hand number by 8 (14) and the right-hand number by 9 (16).

2 DOG – TOWER – HEAD – WALL – CHAIN – BOX **(score 1 point if all correct).**

3 C **(score 1 point).**

4 F **(score 1 point).**
The others pair as follows: A and L; B and K; C and J; D and H; E and I; G and M. The comb does not pair with anything.

5 AF BG CH DE **(score 1 point).**

6 D **(score 1 point).**
The initials are the months of the year. D (December) follows N (November).

7 D **(score 1 point).**
The triangle should be on the right-hand side of the base line.

8 AF BH CG DE **(score 1 point).**
A and F each equal 11.
B and H each equal 13.
C and G each equal 12.
D and E each equal 10.

9 B **(score 1 point).**
In each section the letters in the outer ring combine with those in the inner ring to form a word in conjunction with LAND, which is common to all the words:

IS	LAND	ER
G	LAND	ULAR
OUT	LAND	ISH
UP	LAND	S
S	LAND	ER
GAR	LAND	S
B	LAND	ISHMENT (X is B)

10 **(Score 1 point if all correct; score ½ point if 6 correct).**

PERSONNEL	PROSPERED
OPERATION	STRIPPERS
SUPERSEDE	NEWSPAPER
DESPERATE	

11 AE BD CG FH **(score 1 point).**

12 18 **(score 1 point).**
All the others are divisible by 4.

13 **(score 1 point** for the following, or if you have used other words, provided they are genuine words and fulfil the requirement of changing TWO letters at a time):

```
    R A I N
1   S A I L
2   S N I P
3   S N O W
```

14 (D) **(score 1 point).**
CORINTHIANS is in the New Testament. All the others are in the Old Testament.

15 F and H **(score 1 point if both correct).**

Remember to keep a note of your score.

NOTES

Most time was lost by the volunteers on 1, 2, 8 and 13.

Few were able to solve 1 within the time limit, yet one who was 'pre-tested' arrived at the answer almost immediately. He was a mathematics teacher at a secondary school! The relationship between the numbers outside the brackets and those inside struck him instantly, substantiating the fact that one person will excel in a subject for which a special aptitude is an advantage, whereas another will be stumped by it.

Obviously 8 took some time to solve, as all the mathematical problems had to be solved individually.

The necessity for changing TWO letters at a time created considerable confusion.

TEST 3
(Time limit: 25 minutes)

1 What are x and y?

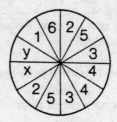

2 Which is the odd one out?
  (A) CABBAGE
  (B) HAPPY
  (C) FELLOW
  (D) KURSAAL
  (E) GLIMMER

3 Complete words to fit the definitions. The number of missing letters is indicated by dashes.

HAPPEN	- - - - - I R E
DRESS	- - - I R E
PLOT	- - - - - I R E
DIE	- - - I R E
WHOLE	- - - I R E
DOMINION	- - - I R E
BOG	- - - - - I R E
LAMPOON	- - - I R E
ARBITRATOR	- - - I R E

4 If is superimposed on

which of the OUTLINES below will result?

A

B

C

D

5 Which column does not conform?

A	B	C	D	E	F
17	14	22	31	29	33
9	13	15	22	19	8
13	11	17	17	31	19
24	7	2	13	5	20
2	29	8	4	2	17
10	6	21	3	10	3

6 If the figure below were held in front of a mirror and the mirror turned upside-down, which of the other figures would be reflected?

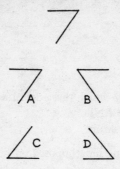

7 Which is the odd one out?
(A) STARLING
(B) PARTRIDGE
(C) GROUSE
(D) BLUETIT
(E) CUCKOO-PINT
(F) LARK
(G) NIGHTINGALE

8 Which row is wrong?

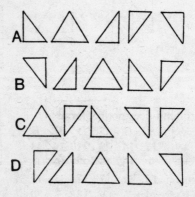

9 What is two days after the day after the day before yesterday?

10 Which is the odd word out?

(A) MEDICAL
(B) BATTLE
(C) ARTICLE
(D) BALLET
(E) RECITAL
(F) CLAIMED
(G) TABLET

11 Give words for which these definitions are given. Each word must contain AND.

(A) Evergreen shrub
(B) Lizard-like animal
(C) Stray
(D) Footwear
(E) Baton
(F) Part of Scotland
(G) Sweetmeat
(H) Make love triflingly
(I) Spend wastefully
(J) Strainer

12 Which trellis is wrong?

13 If 3 (76) equals 212
and 4 (320) equals 125
what is:
     5 (6100) ?

31

14 **Without turning the page**, which of these numbers
will **not** read the same when turned upside-down?

A 8|69|8

B 8|8|8

C |8998|

D ||69||

E |96961

15 One of these words is spelt wrongly. Which one?
  (A) RECEIVE
  (B) IMMANENT
  (C) FASCIA
  (D) DESSICATED
  (E) BUDGERIGAR
  (F) SCHISM
  (G) PNEUMONIA
  (H) NASCENT
  (I) LEMUR
  (J) CHEETAH

**Now check your answers and keep a note of your
score.**

ANSWERS

1 x is 6; y is 1 **(score 1 point if both correct)**.
Starting at No 1 and moving to alternate segments clockwise:

$$1 \; 2 \; 3 \; 4 \; 5 \; 6$$

Starting at No 6 and moving in the same way:

$$6 \; 5 \; 4 \; 3 \; 2 \; 1$$

2 (D) **(score 1 point)**.
In KURSAAL there are two identical adjacent vowels. In all the other words there are two identical adjacent consonants.

3 **(Score 1 point if all correct; $\frac{1}{2}$ if 7 or 8)**.

TRANSPIRE	EMPIRE
ATTIRE	QUAGMIRE
CONSPIRE	SATIRE
EXPIRE	UMPIRE
ENTIRE	

4 B **(score 1 point)**.

5 E **(score 1 point)**.
Adding up each column:

Column A ... 75	Column D ... 90
Column B ... 80	Column E ... *96*
Column C ... 85	Column F ... 100

6 B **(score 1 point)**.
The fact that the MIRROR (not the figure!) is held upside-down will make no difference to the reflection.

7 (E) **(score 1 point)**.
CUCKOO-PINT is a flower – the common arum or the wake-robin. All the others are birds.

8   C **(score 1 point).**
   Except for C, each row contains 1 equilateral triangle, 2 right-angled triangles with the base at the bottom and 2 with the base at the top.
   In C there are 3 right-angled triangles with the base at the top and only one with the base at the bottom.

9   Tomorrow **(score 1 point).**
   The day before yesterday was two days ago; the day after the day before yesterday was yesterday; two days after that (yesterday) is TOMORROW.

10   (D) **(score 1 point).**
   Apart from this, the words are paired in anagrams:
   (A) MEDICAL with (F) CLAIMED
   (B) BATTLE with (G) TABLET
   (C) ARTICLE with (E) RECITAL
   No word listed forms an anagram with BALLET.

11   **(Score 1 point if all correct; $\frac{1}{2}$ if 8 or 9).**
   (A)   OLEANDER
   (B)   SALAMANDER
   (C)   WANDER
   (D)   SANDAL
   (E)   WAND
   (F)   HIGHLANDS or LOWLANDS
   (G)   CANDY
   (H)   PHILANDER
   (I)   SQUANDER
   (J)   COLANDER

12   E **(score 1 point).**
   The diagonal slat from top left to bottom right should pass under the other slats.

13 3020 **(score 1 point).**

The first two digits on the right of the brackets are divided by the digit on the left to give the first digit inside the brackets.

The remaining number on the right of the brackets is multiplied by the digit on the left of the brackets to give the remaining number inside the brackets.

14 C **(score 1 point).**

15 (D) **(score 1 point).**

This should be spelt: DESICCATED.

Remember to keep a note of your score.

NOTES

Questions 3 and 11 called for a fair amount of writing, which is allowed for in the time limit.

A few volunteers were caught out by 6, jumping at what *appeared* to be the obvious, but overlooking the vital fact that the reversal of the mirror makes no difference to the reflection.

Many lost points on 7 and 11; in the latter, (A), (B), (H) and (J) caused most trouble.

In 15 the fairly well-recognised general weakness in spelling was revealed. Remarkably, two *chefs* failed to spot that DESICCATED was spelt wrongly!

TEST 4
(Time limit: 30 minutes)

1 Which of the symbols at the bottom should take the place of X?

)(　()　◡　≍

()　◡　≍　)(

◡　≍　)(　()
　　　　　　　X

A　B　C　D
◡　≍　()　)(

2 What is X?

2　1　8　5　9
3　7　2　6　2
4　2　1　1　X

3 Supply the missing letter. (Proper nouns not allowed!)

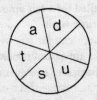

4 Which is the odd one out?
  (A) SHORE   (C) TUTOR
  (B) KEPI   (D) ACED

5 Which letter does not conform with the others?

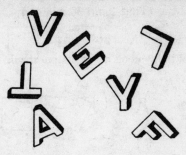

6 What WORD is represented by X?

31   31   X   31

7 Which is the odd one out?
  (A) TESTAMENT
  (B) PROMINENCE
  (C) FILAMENT
  (D) GRAVAMEN
  (E) FLAMENCO
  (F) STAMENS

8 Give words to fit these definitions. Each word must contain part of the body:
  (A) Apparatus for applying mechanical power.
  (B) Fast time for a musician.
  (C) Gardener's means of transport.
  (D) Uttering of speech.
  (E) Nautical pal.
  (F) Mixed drink.

37

9 Arrange these into six pairs:

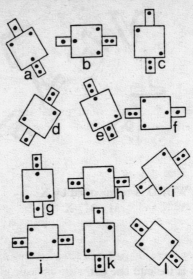

10 What is X?

3 6 10 15 X 28

11 Give words to satisfy the definitions. Each word must start with the last two letters of the previous word.

(A) STAR
(B) FISH
(C) END OF THE LINE
(D) CUSTOMARY PRACTICE
(E) ARMY OFFICER
(F) SEPARATION ALLOWANCE
(G) SYNTHETIC FIBRE
(H) ATTACK
(I) WORDY FELLOW!
(J) THOROUGHFARE

12 Which are the weak links?

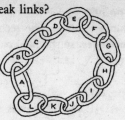

13 The same four-letter word placed inside the brackets will complete the words.

A (– – – –) N T
S U B (– – – –)
(– – – –) R I C K

14 What are X and Y?

7 8 6 9 5 10 X Y 3 12

15 Arrange these shapes in order according to the number of sides, starting with the one with the least number:

(A) OCTAGON   (E) TETRAGON
(B) HEXAGON   (F) NONAGON
(C) PENTAGON   (G) HEPTAGON
(D) DECAGON

Now check your answers and keep a note of your score.

ANSWERS

1 A (score 1 point).

In each row the first symbol is the same as the second in the previous row and the other symbols continue in the same order.

39

2 2 **(score 1 point).**

The first column totals 9. The second column totals 10. This pattern continues, so the final column should total 13, by the addition of *2*.

3 J **(score 1 point).**

The word is: ADJUST. (Datsun is not allowed.)

4 (A) **(score 1 point).**

An anagram of HORSE. All the others are anagrams of fishes:
- (B) PIKE
- (C) TROUT
- (D) DACE

5 L **(score 1 point).**

The block (the black portion) should be on the right of the letter.

6 SEPTEMBER **(score 1 point).**

These are obviously the number of days in the months. September is the only month which has two 31-day months before it and one after it.

7 (B) **(score 1 point).**

All the other words contain AMEN.

8 **(Score 1 point if all correct; $\frac{1}{2}$ if 5 correct).**
- (A) maCHINe
- (B) alLEGro
- (C) wHEELbarrow
- (D) deLIVERy
- (E) sHIPmate
- (F) sHANDy

9 ag ci bf dk ej hl **(score 1 point).**

10   21 **(score 1 point)**.
   The numbers increase by 3, 4, 5, 6 and 7

11   **(Score 1 point if all correct; ½ if 8 or 9 correct)**.
   asteriSK   ALimoNY
   SKaTE   NYlON
   TErminUS   ONsET
   USaGE   ETymologiST
   GEnerAL   STreet

12   G and H **(score 1 point)**.

13   LIME **(score 1 point)**.
   The words are:
   aliment
   sublime
   limerick

14   X is 4; Y is 11 **(score 1 point if both correct)**.
   Two alternate series
   Starting with the first number: 7 6 5 *4* 3
   Starting with the second number: 8 9 10 *11* 12

15   **(Score 1 point if all correct; ½ if 6 correct)**.
   (E)   TETRAGON — 4 sides
   (C)   PENTAGON — 5 sides
   (B)   HEXAGON — 6 sides
   (G)   HEPTAGON — 7 sides
   (A)   OCTAGON — 8 sides
   (F)   NONAGON — 9 sides
   (D)   DECAGON — 10 sides

Keep a note of your score.
   Now total up your scores for the first four tests and
compare them with the ratings that follow.

NOTES

Two of the problems – 8 and 11 – require fairly long written answers (allowed for in the time limit).

The volunteers experienced most difficulty with 8, 11 and 15.

RATINGS IN GROUP I

TEST 1 ..... Average $8\frac{1}{2}$ points
TEST 2 ..... Average $7\frac{1}{2}$ points
TEST 3 ..... Average 10 points
TEST 4 ..... Average 9 points

Total for the Group

Out of a possible 60 points:
Over 52 ..... Excellent
46 – 52 ..... Very good
36 – 45 ..... Good
35 ..... Average
30 – 34 ..... Fair
Under 30 ..... Poor

Especially if you scored 26 or under, it is suggested that you go through the problems again, in conjunction with the answers and explanations, so that you will have a better understanding of the tests to follow.

GROUP II
MORE DIFFICULT

TEST 1
(Time limit: 20 minutes)

1 Solve the clues, and two boys' names will appear in the vertical columns headed x and y.

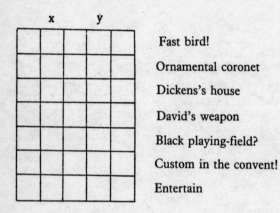

x   ẏ

Fast bird!

Ornamental coronet

Dickens's house

David's weapon

Black playing-field?

Custom in the convent!

Entertain

2 Which triangle is wrong?

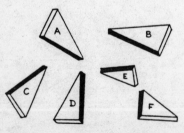

44

3 Square the third lowest even number and subtract the result from the third highest odd number:

$$
\begin{array}{cccccc}
9 & 67 & 4 & 11 & 58 & 66 \\
2 & 65 & 1 & 8 & 10 & 41 \\
6 & 71 & 5 & 12 & 25 & 3 \\
7 & 41 & 32 & 70 & 69 & 68
\end{array}
$$

4 Which is the odd one out?
  (A) FEDERATION
  (B) OUTSPAN
  (C) CANOPY
  (D) COUPON
  (E) ABUTS
  (F) REDCAP

5 What should go into the empty segment?

6 Whose face is in the mirror?

7 What is X?

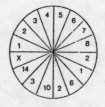

8 TWO different words can be made by inserting two different letters into the blank space. You must give both words.

9 Which words go into the brackets? Each word must logically follow the previous word and precede the next word, e.g. putting (GREEN) fingers.

COMMON
(A) (   )
GARDEN
(B) (   )
SPIRIT
(C) (   )
BEST
(D) (   )
SLAUGHTER
(E) (   )
BOAT
(F) (   )
HORSE
(G) (   )
BLACK
(H) (   )
DOG
(I) (   )
WOOD
(J) (   )
TOED

10 Which of the numbered circles at the bottom should be placed at A, B, C and D?

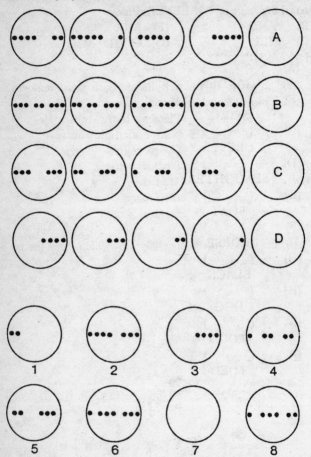

11 What is the difference between the lowest number and the *average* of all the numbers?

3   9   12   15   18   25   30

12 Here are seven common words. Which is the odd one out?

(A) DIM
(B) MIND
(C) MILL
(D) LIVID
(E) VIM
(F) MIX
(G) CIVIL

13 Give words to fit the definitions. Each word removes one letter from the word above it.

$-\ -\ -\ -\ -\ -$ —Place for burnt stubs
$-\ -\ -\ -\ -\ -$ Not on the right course
$-\ -\ -\ -\ -$ Go off course
$-\ -\ -\ -$ Shallow vessel
$-\ -\ -$ Sea-fish
$-\ -$ Affirmative
$-$ Musical note

14 Can you make an identikit picture? Which three pieces below will make the face above?

15   What is X?

**Now check your answers and keep a note of your
score.**

ANSWERS

1   x is WILLIAM: y is FRANCIS **(score 1 point if both
correct).**

s	W	i	F	t
t	I	a	R	a
b	L	e	A	k
s	L	i	N	g
p	I	t	C	h
h	A	b	I	t
a	M	u	S	e

2   F **(score 1 point).**
  The shorter side is shaded. In all the other triangles the
longer side is shaded.

3   31 **(score 1 point).**

4   (C) **(score 1 point).**
  CANOPY contains three consecutive letters in their
correct order. All the other words contain three consecutive
letters in reverse order.

5 elbi **(score 1 point; if you have answered ible score $\frac{1}{2}$ point)**.

Each word starts with COM.

The syllables that follow are read *backwards* in the outer sections:

COM – FORT – ABLE
COM – MAN – DO
COM – MISER – ATE
COM – PARIS – ON
COM – PAT – RIOT
COM – EST – IBLE (the only possible syllable to make a word)

6 A **(score 1 point)**.

7 4 **(score 1 point)**.

Moving clockwise and starting with No 1 in the upper half, compare each number with that in its opposite segment. 1 is doubled, giving 2 in the opposite segment; the next number (2) is halved giving 1 in the opposite segment. The same procedure continues: double the next, then halve the next.

8 in the upper half is halved to give *4* in the opposite segment.

(An alternative solution is to double all the odd numbers and halve all the even numbers).

8 E (ENEMY) and O (MONEY) **(score 1 point if both correct)**.

9 **(Score 1 point if all correct; $\frac{1}{2}$ if 8 or 9 correct)**.

(A) MARKET	(F) RACE	
(B) PARTY	(G) SHOE	
(C) LEVEL	(H) WATCH	
(D) MAN	(I) ROSE	
(E) HOUSE	(J) PIGEON	

10 A 3; B 6; C 1; D 7 (**score 1 point if all correct; $\frac{1}{2}$ if 3 correct**).

Careful examination of the spots indicates the direction of rotation.

The first row rotates from left to right;
the second row rotates from right to left;
the third row rotates from right to left;
the fourth row rotates from left to right.

11 13 (**score 1 point**).

12 (B) (**score 1 point**).

All the other words are made up with Roman numerals. N is not a Roman numeral.

13 (**Score 1 point if all correct**).

```
A S H T R A Y
A S T R A Y
S T R A Y
T R A Y
R A Y
A Y
A
```

14 b, e and h (**score 1 point if all correct**).

15 140 (**score 1 point**).

Starting with 3 in the upper half, the number in the opposite segment multiplies it by 2. The next number (7) is multiplied by 3; then by 4, and so on.

Therefore 20 is multiplied by 7 to give *140*.

Remember to keep a note of your score.

NOTES

In 6 it was not always realised by the volunteers that stripes in the tie are diagonally reversed in a mirror reflection.

Nos 7 and 15 seemed to give the greatest difficulty, though much time was lost (not always to good purpose) over No. 9.

TEST 2
(Time limit: 40 minutes)

1 Which cup is the odd one out?

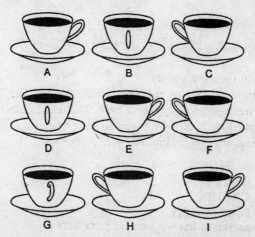

2   What is the TOTAL of the spots on the rear side?

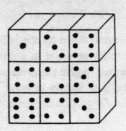

3   The same four letters in a different order will complete these words:

(A)   – – – – t e d
(B)   l – – – –
(C)   – – – – t
(D)   e y – – – – l
(E)   c u l p – – – –

4   What comes next?
         124   81   6   32   641   2   –

5   Which is the odd one out?
(A)   HEARD
(B)   RUSHING
(C)   CLIPPER
(D)   URCHIN
(E)   DIAGNOSED
(F)   MONEYED

6 What are a, b, c and d?
                3 27 1 32 4 26 3 29
                5 25 5 26 6 a b c d

7 What letter should go into the empty space?

8 What letters should be substituted for X and Y on the last cube?

9   If this shape were folded along the dotted lines it could be made into a cube:

like this:

If this cube is turned upside-down, which of these faces will appear at the top?

A   B   C

10   What are x, y and z?

A 1 3 L 12 6 M 13 9
0 15 12 S 19 x y z

11   The same word can precede each of these words:
   (A) CASE
   (B) BOY
   (C) TON
   (D) GO
   (E) APACE

12 Examine the first three car number-plates and then complete the last one:

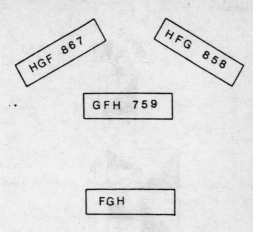

HGF 867

HFG 858

GFH 759

FGH

13 What are x, y and z?

3	42	40
7	52	53
12	63	68
18	75	85
25	88	104
X	102	125
42	Y	148
52	133	Z

14 If this design were turned 90 degrees anti-clockwise and held in front of a mirror, which of the designs below would be reflected?

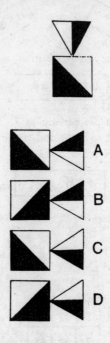

15 All of these might be found on a railway station, but you must unscramble them first:
  (A) REPORT
  (B) PRAM LOFT
  (C) TOOK BALLS
  (D) LINE STOMACH (two words)
  (E) YET ROLL

Now check your answers and keep a note of your score.

ANSWERS

1 **G (score 1 point).**
The handle is in the wrong position, as compared with B and D.

2 **29 (score 1 point).**
Opposite faces of a die add up to 7. Therefore, moving horizontally from left to right and starting in the top row, opposite faces are: 6 4 1 3 5 2 1 3 4

3 B A L E (in any order) **(score 1 point if all correct; ½ point if 4 correct).**
The words become:
(A) *BELA*TED
(B) *L*ABEL
(C) *BLEA*T
(D) EYE*BALL*
(E) CULP*ABLE*

4 **8 (score 1 point).**
This is an ordinary 'doubling-up' series, but wrongly spaced. When correctly spaced, the answer becomes obvious: 1 2 4 8 16 32 64 12*8*

5 **(B) (score 1 point).**
This contains SHIN – part of the leg. All the others contain parts of the head or face:
(A) HEARD – contains EAR
(C) CLIPPER – contains LIP
(D) URCHIN – contains CHIN
(E) DIAGNOSED – contains NOSE
(F) MONEYED – contains EYE

59

6   a is 24; b is 7; c is 23; d is 7 **(score 1 point if all correct; ½ point if 2 or 3 correct)**.

There are four series. Starting with the first term and taking every fourth term thereafter:

3   4   5   6   7(d)

Starting with the second term and continuing in the same way:

27   26   25   24(a)

Starting with the third term:

1   3   5   7(b)

Starting with the fourth term:

32   29   26   23(c)

7   Q **(score 1 point)**.

The word is REQUIEM.

8   x is I; y is Q **(score 1 point if both correct; ½ point if one correct)**.

The front face of each cube advances the letter on the right face by four positions in the alphabet. The top face advances the front face by three positions on the first cube, then by four positions, then by five positions, and so on. (Alternatively: increase the top faces by 7 positions at a time, the other faces by 6 positions at a time).

9   C **(score 1 point)**.

10   x is 15; y is T; z is 20 **(score 1 point if all correct; ½ if 2 correct)**.

There are three series.

Starting with the first term and taking every third term thereafter: A L M O S — The only letter that will complete a word is T (ALMOST) — represented by y. The number that follows each letter represents the position in the alphabet of that letter. Therefore, T — represented by y —

should be followed by 20 (T is the 20th letter) — the value for z.

Starting with the third term and taking every third term thereafter: 3 6 9 12 15 (the value for x).

11 CAR (score 1 point).
The words become:
(A) CARCASE
(B) CARBOY
(C) CARTON
(D) CARGO
(E) CARAPACE

12 669 (score 1 point).
All the first three number-plates follow the same pattern.

The first letter gives the first digit (H is 8 — its position in the alphabet).

The second letter gives the second digit by reducing its alphabetical position by 1 (G — the 7th letter becomes 6).

The third letter gives the third digit by increasing its alphabetical position by 1 (F becomes 7, increasing its 6th position by 1).

Therefore, in the final number-plate:
F gives 6 (the 6th letter)
G gives 6 (reducing the 7th letter by one)
H gives 9 (increasing the 8th letter by one).

13 x is 33; y is 117; z is 173 (score 1 point if all correct; ½ if 2 correct).
Moving down in the left-hand vertical column, the numbers increase by 4, 5, 6 and so on. 25 should be increased by 8 to give 33 — the value for x.

The middle vertical column increases by 10, 11, 12 and so on. 102 should be increased by 15 to give 117 — the value for y.

The right-hand vertical column increases progressively —
13, 15, 17, 19 and so on. 148 should be increased by 25 to
give 173 — the value for z.

14   A (score 1 point).

15   (Score 1 point if all correct; $\frac{1}{2}$ point if 4 correct).
   (A)   PORTER
   (B)   PLATFORM
   (C)   BOOKSTALL
   (D)   SLOT MACHINE
   (E)   TROLLEY

Remember to keep a note of your score.

NOTES

Definitely the most difficult test so far, which produced very
low scores for the volunteers.

Questions 6 and 10 gave examples of the 'multiple series'
type of question, that is two or more series embraced in an
overall series, where every second, third or fourth term has
to be considered. It is well to become accustomed to this type
of question as you *may* find more based on the same
principle later.

No 4 was an example of a simple series incorrectly spaced.
Again, you *may* come across similar problems later.

Because of the complicated thinking involved, the time
limit was extended to compensate.

Questions 4, 6, 8 and 12 gave the greatest difficulty.

In the case of No 11, if you were familiar with the word
CARAPACE — the shell of a tortoise or crustacean — this
should have provided you with a vital clue as to the missing
word. Failing that knowledge, possibly GO was the next best
lead to bring you to the answer.

TEST 3
(Time limit: 22 minutes)

1 Which is the odd one out?
   (A) IAMBUS
   (B) TROCHEE
   (C) RONDURE
   (D) PAEON
   (E) SPONDEE
   (F) DACTYL

2 Which one is different?

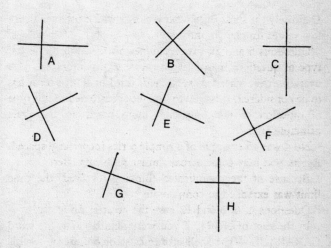

3 What comes next in this series?

16 72 38 94 50 –

4 The black ball moves one position at a time clockwise.
  The white ball moves two positions at a time anti-clockwise.
  a) In how many moves will they be together again?
  b) In what corner will they be?

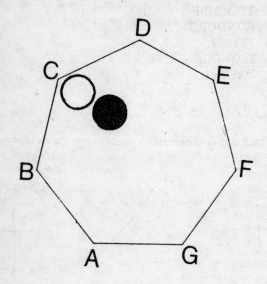

5 What is X?

1	2	3	4	5	6	7	8
7	14	1	2	2	1	8	7
10	3	4	18	2	1	8	6
8	5	11	12	2	21	3	4
2	11	6	3	13	1	2	10
2	5	5	1	6	10	2	X

6 A sentence may conceal a 'hidden' word. Thus, in this sentence the word ENSIGN is 'hidden': Heath*ENS IGN*ore Christians.

What 'voices' are hidden in these sentences?

(A) 'Parsifal,' set to music, is very popular.

(B) Mr. Allsop ran on to win the race.

(C) They often organise concerts.

(D) Rumbas, sambas and waltzes are my favourite dances.

(E) The total tonnage is ten thousand.

7 If the two dotted lines are placed together, what will be the result?

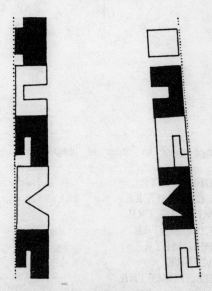

8   What are x and y?

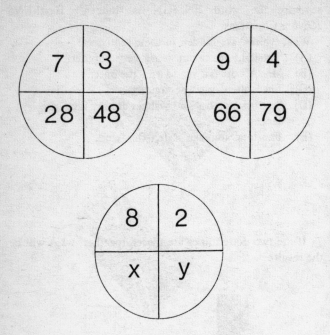

9   Arrange these in order of length, starting with the shortest:
- (A) DECAMETRE
- (B) CENTIMETRE
- (C) MILLIMETRE
- (D) KILOMETRE
- (E) DECIMETRE
- (F) METRE
- (G) HECTOMETRE

10 Which flag is wrong — and WHY?

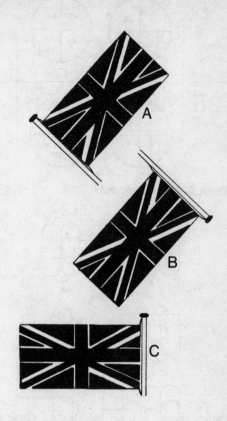

11 Who is the odd man out?
  (A) MARCONI
  (B) CARUSO
  (C) EDISON
  (D) BAIRD
  (E) ARKWRIGHT

12 What are x and y?

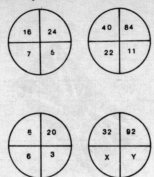

13 Which is the odd one out?

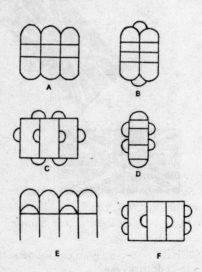

14 What comes next in this series?
1072 1055 1021 953 817 545 –

15 Complete the final square:

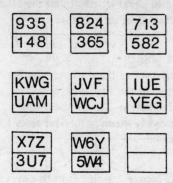

| 935 | 824 | 713 |
| 148 | 365 | 582 |

| KWG | JVF | IUE |
| UAM | WCJ | YEG |

| X7Z | W6Y | |
| 3U7 | 5W4 | |

Now check your answers and keep a note of your score.

ANSWERS

1 (C) **(score 1 point)**.

RONDURE is a round outline or object.

All the others are metrical feet:

(A)	IAMBUS	–a short accent followed by a long one;
(B)	TROCHEE	–a long accent followed by a short one;
(D)	PAEON	–a long accent (placed anywhere) and three short ones;
(E)	SPONDEE	–two long accents;
(F)	DACTYL	–a long accent followed by two short ones.

69

2 D **(score 1 point).**

The lines are of equal length. In all the others one line is longer (or shorter) than the other.

3 16 **(score 1 point).**

Each number reverses the previous number and adds 1 to each digit. Thus, in the first two terms, 16 reversed is 61, which then changes to 72. In the penultimate term, 50 reversed becomes 05, which in turn becomes 16 — by adding 1 to each digit.

4 (A) 7; (B) C **(score 1 point if both correct; $\frac{1}{2}$ point if one correct).**

	Black ball	White ball
1st move	D	A
2nd move	E	F
3rd move	F	D
4th move	G	B
5th move	A	G
6th move	B	E
7th move	*C*	*C*

5 5 **(score 1 point).**

Columns headed by an odd number add up to 30. Columns headed by an even number add up to 40. The last column adds up to 35, to which must be added 5 to bring it up to 40, as this column is headed by an even number.

6 **(Score 1 point if all correct; $\frac{1}{2}$ point if 4 correct).**

(A) FALSETTO
(B) SOPRANO
(C) TENOR
(D) BASS
(E) ALTO

7 THEME **(score 1 point).**

This is the result of placing them together:

8 x is 11; y is 61 **(score 1 point if both correct; ½ point if one correct).**

In the first circle the number in the top left quarter is squared and then reduced by 1 in the opposite diagonal quarter; the number in the top right quarter is cubed and then 1 added to give the number in the opposite lower quarter.

In the second circle the same procedure is followed, except that 2 is deducted from the squared number and 2 is added to the cubed number.

Therefore, in the third circle *3* is deducted from the square of 8 (64 becomes 61 — the value for y), while *3* is added to the cube of 2 (8 becomes 11 — the value for x).

9 **(Score 1 point if all correct; ½ point if 6 correct).**
   (C) MILLIMETRE
   (B) CENTIMETRE
   (E) DECIMETRE
   (F) METRE
   (A) DECAMETRE
   (G) HECTOMETRE
   (D) KILOMETRE

10 C — because it is flying upside-down! **(Score 1 point — but only if you have given the correct reason).**

If you have answered D because it is flying on the left of the flagstaff, this cannot be accepted, since it is immaterial which side it is flying (the wind is probably blowing in the opposite direction!)

The Union Jack (or Union Flag) should be flown with the broad white stripe nearest to the flagstaff uppermost. To fly it with the narrow white stripe uppermost is a sign of distress.

11 (B) (score 1 point).

Caruso was a singer. All the others were inventors.

12 x is 9 or 24; y also is 9 or 24 (score 1 point if both correct).

In each case the numbers at the top are divided by 4 in the opposite quarter and 1 is added.

An alternative solution is that the numbers in the lower quarters are multiplied by 4 in their opposite quarters and 4 is deducted from the result.

13 C (score 1 point).

In C there are 8 curves and 6 straight lines. In all the others there are 6 curves and 6 straight lines.

14 1 (score 1 point).

The numbers reduce by 17, 34, 68, 136, 272 and hence — 544 thus reducing the previous number — 545 by 1. (The terms reduce in multiples of 17.)

15 (Score 1 point).

In the top line throughout, whether using letters or numbers, they reduce by one position in each successive square.

In the bottom line it has been established that they

increase by two positions, *except for the last term*, which reduces its position by *three* places from that in the previous square.

Remember to keep a note of your score.

NOTES

The numerical problems seemed to give our volunteers the greatest difficulty — 3, 5 and 14 particularly, though 5 was based more on logical thinking than numeracy in itself.

Few succeeded with No 1 and, surprisingly (now that the decimal and metric systems have taken over) No 9 brought several defeats, even though (B), (C), (F) and (D) were rightly placed.

Sad to say, in No 10, the fact that the Union Flag was flying upside-down in C was relegated in favour of the (invalid) fact that it was on the other side of the flagstaff.

TEST 4

(Time limit: 45 minutes)
(You may rest after 25 minutes and
then resume for 20 minutes)

1 What is x?

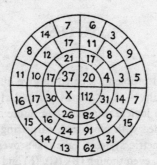

2 Which one is wrong?

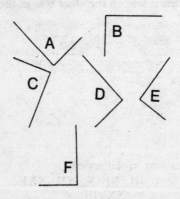

3 Which of the figures at the bottom should follow the six figures at the top?

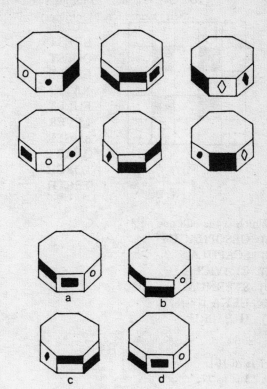

4 What comes next in this series?

I III VI X XV XXI
XXVIII –

5 Complete this crossword puzzle, choosing words from the list below:

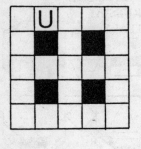

TULIP
BURST
QUEST
EAGLE
RATIO
FULLY
LEVER
ANGER
QUART
TORCH
TEETH

6 Which is the odd one out?
  (A) OESOPHAGUS
  (B) SCAPULA
  (C) CLAVICLE
  (D) STERNUM
  (E) ULNA
  (F) HUMERUS

7 17 is to 101
  as 13 is to 77,
  and as 19 is to .....?

8 Join these words to form ten other words or words which pair together:

TEN	DEN	ORC	MATE	LIGHT
SCHOOL	SUN	HOME	HID	DON
WAY	DAY	HIGH	KEY	BOY
SHIP	MON	HELP	HARD	CHECK

9 Which currency belongs to which country?
  (A) KRONE   (1) SPAIN
  (B) LIRA   (2) DENMARK
  (C) PESETA   (3) PORTUGAL
  (D) ESCUDO   (4) RUSSIA
  (E) ROUBLE   (5) ITALY

10

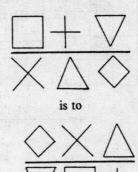

is to

$$\frac{351}{762}$$

is to
?

11 What comes next in this series?

	1		0		11		E		8		E		12		T
		2		T		3		T		4		–			

77

12 All of these shapes — except one — are of the same area.
Which is the exception, and is it of greater or lesser area?

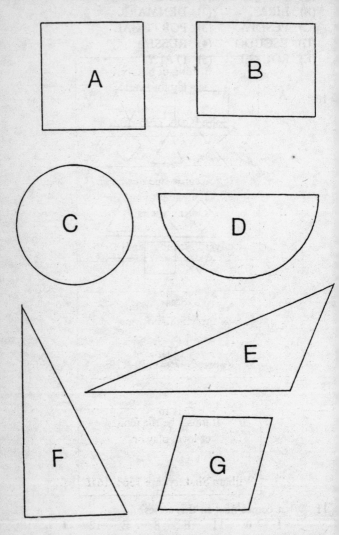

13   Which of these is wrong?

A

A thing of beauty
is a joy for ever.

John Keats 1795–1821

B

If you can keep your head
when all about you/Are
losing theirs.

Rudyard Kipling 1865–1936

C

My heart's in the
the Highlands, my
heart is not here.

Robert Burns 1739–1796

D

If music be the food
of love, play on.

William Shakespeare 1564–1616

14   What does the third clock show?

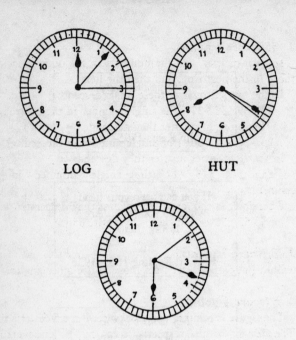

LOG   HUT

15   Which number is nearest to the number which is
midway between the lowest and the highest number?

11	84	41	9	79
81	7	36	51	47
88	12	8	89	10

**Now check your answers and keep a note of your
score.**

ANSWERS

1 55 (score 1 point).
In each quarter, add the numbers in the outer ring, then those in the next ring, and then the next.
In the top left quarter these totals descend:
   40 39 38 37 (the single number in the centre).
In the top right quarter they descend:
   23 22 21 20 (the single number in the centre).
In the right lower quarter they descend:
   115 114 113 112 (the single number in the centre).
Therefore, in the lower left quarter they descend:
   58 57 56 — and then, obviously, *55* (x).

2 E (score 1 point).
Both lines are shorter than those in the other angles.

3 a (score 1 point).
The figure is rotating anti-clockwise, three faces at a time. The designs on the respective faces can be discovered by examining the figures at the top, which are in this sequence:

4 XXXVI (score 1 point).
First change the Roman numerals into modern numerals:
   1 3 6 10 15 21 28
It can be seen that the terms increase by:
   2, 3, 4, 5, 6 and 7.
Hence the final number must increase the previous one by 8 (28 increases to 36, or *XXXVI* in Roman numerals).

5   Either of these solutions **scores 1 point**.

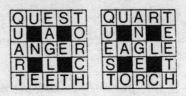

6   (A) **(score 1 point)**.

OESOPHAGUS is the canal from the mouth to the stomach, or the gullet.

All the others are bones:

(B)   SCAPULA — shoulder-blade

(C)   CLAVICLE — collar-bone

(D)   STERNUM — breast-bone

(E)   ULNA — inner bone of the forearm

(F)   HUMERUS — bone of the upper arm

7   113 **(score 1 point)**.

In each case the number is multiplied by 6 and 1 is subtracted from the result.

8   **(Score 1 point if all correct; ½ point if 8 or 9 correct)**.

TEN	DON
MON	KEY
ORC	HARD
HID	DEN
SUN	DAY
LIGHT	SHIP
CHECK	MATE
HOME	HELP
HIGH	WAY
SCHOOL	BOY

9 (A) (2); (B) (5); (C) (1); (D) (3); (E) (4) **(score 1 point if all correct).**

10 **(Score 1 point).**

$$\frac{276}{135}$$

11 **F (score 1 point).**
   Each letter is the initial letter of the previous number, hence 4 (FOUR) is followed by *F*.

12 G is of LESSER area than the others, which are all of the same area. **(Score 1 point).**

13 **C (score 1 point).**
   The definite article (THE) is repeated in the second line.

14 **FIR (score 1 point).**
   The first letter is indicated by the position of the hour hand relative to the hours — in this case 6, that is the sixth letter (F).
   The next letter is shown by the position of the second hand. Here it is on the 9th second, and the ninth letter is I.
   The third letter is indicated by the position of the minute hand. As it points to the 18th minute, it shows that the third letter is R — the 18th letter in the alphabet.

15 **36 (score 1 point).**

Keep a note of your score.
   Now total up your scores for the four tests and compare them with the ratings that follow.

NOTES

A difficult test, which did not receive high scores among our volunteers.

Questions 1, 2, 4 and 9 gained the most correct answers, but 3 and 5 might have had you really puzzled.

In 13 it was surprisingly easy to overlook the fact that the definite article was repeated. When a book (such as this!) is in the proof stage before receiving its final printing, it is the job of the proof-reader to spot any solecisms — which creep in insidiously, however careful the printer has been. Proof-reading is itself a very specialised job, and yet, surprisingly, it is easy enough to overlook a printing error — as witness from those who failed to spot this one.

Probably those who did not answer this correctly were concentrating too much on the authors and the dates, suspecting that there was a factual error here, when, in fact, the authors and the dates of their lifetimes were correctly quoted.

RATINGS IN GROUP II

TEST 1 ..... Average 7 points
TEST 2 ..... Average $5\frac{1}{2}$ points
TEST 3 ..... Average 8 points
TEST 4 ..... Average $5\frac{1}{2}$ points

Total for the Group

Out of a possible 60 points:

Over 48	..... Excellent
40 – 47	..... Very good
27 – 39	..... Good
26	..... Average
20 – 25	..... Fair
Under 20	..... Poor

Although most of these problems were more difficult than those in the previous group, a score of under 20 implies that you should try to acquire a better understanding of these types of tests. It would be a good idea to go again right through all the problems up to here, in conjunction with the answers. As the final ratings — given at the end of all three groups — are the all-important ones for assessing your *overall* comprehension, do not lose heart yet if your scores to date are low. You may still make up lost ground in the final (difficult) group which follows.

GROUP III
DIFFICULT

TEST 1

(Time limit: 1 hour 15 minutes)
(You may rest after 45 minutes and
then resume for a further 30 minutes)

1 Complete these words, using all the letters contained in
this ungrammatical sentence:

HERE IS TEN FAT CATTLE
(A) – E – R – S – M – N –
(B) – R – N – P – R – N –
(C) – O – T – N – N – A –

2 Which of the lower circles should take the place of No 5?

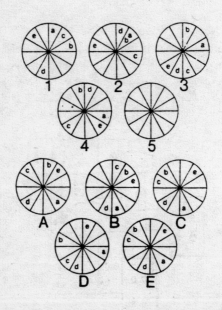

3 When a dart lands in an even number the next throw lands it in the second odd number clockwise.

When a dart lands in an odd number the next throw lands it in the third even number clockwise from the previous throw.

As can be seen, the first dart has already been thrown.

Four more darts are to be thrown. What will be the total score of the five darts?

4 What famous author is this?

5 What letter starts the last word?

P A T C H

K I N K

T E A S

- . E N D

6 A clock shows 9.25. If it were held upside-down in front of a mirror, which of those below would be reflected?

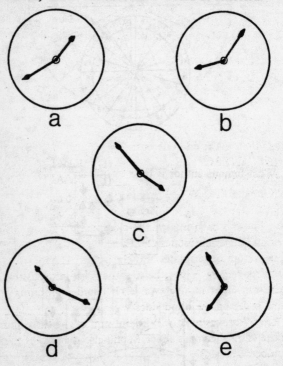

a

b

c

d

e

7 Which number in the bottom line should come next in the top line?

15 16 21 20 9 88 18 28 –

7 34 19 17 22 66

8 Find words for A, B, C, D, E, F, G and H:

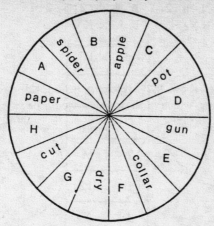

9 Which is the odd one out?

(A) ANZAC
(B) NATO
(C) PLUTO
(D) KIWI
(E) NAAFI

10 The top band rotates anti-clockwise.
The middle band rotates clockwise.
The bottom band rotates anti-clockwise.
Each movement brings the next number into position, and there are eight numbers on each band, continuing in the same order on the blind sides.

After 7 moves what will be the sum of the three numbers in the vertical column above A, and also the sum of the three numbers above B?

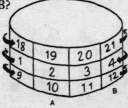

11 What comes next here?

    1 8 2 7 6 4 1 2 5 2 1 –

12 What is X?

T	0
18	B
O	5
7	M
H	12
19	A
X	2

13 Which of the numbered figures at the bottom should take the places of A, B and C?

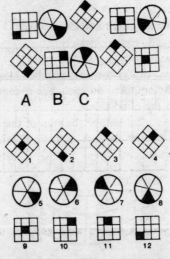

92

14 What is x?

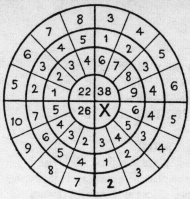

15 A advances 1 place, then 2, then 3, etc., increasing its jump by one each time.

B advances 2 places, then 3, then 4, etc., increasing its jump by one each time.

C advances 3 places, then 4, then 5, etc., increasing its jump by one each time.

Which will be the first to reach 25 EXACTLY?

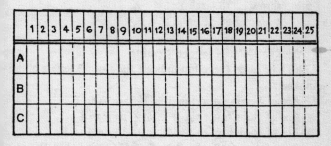

	1	2	3	4	5	6	7	8	9	10	11	12	13	14	15	16	17	18	19	20	21	22	23	24	25
A																									
B																									
C																									

Now check your answers and keep a note of your score.

ANSWERS

1 (Score 1 point if all correct).
  (A) REFRESHMENT
  (B) TRANSPARENT
  (C) CONTINENTAL

2 E (score 1 point).
  a moves one place at a time clockwise;
  b moves one place at a time anti-clockwise;
  c moves two places at a time clockwise;
  d moves to and from opposite segments;
  e moves anti-clockwise, first one place, then two, then
    three, and so on.

3 68 (score 1 point).
  1st throw ... 18
  2nd throw ... 15
  3rd throw ... 8
  4th throw ... 9
  5th throw ... 18 (again)
        Total 68

4 MARK TWAIN (score 1 point).
The four cards at the top indicate the first 23 letters of the
alphabet:
    Ace of hearts up to the 5 ... 1–5, or A to E
    Ace of clubs up to the 4 ... 6–9, or F to I
    Ace of spades up to the 7 ... 10–16, or J to P
    Ace of diamonds up to the 7 ... 17–23, or Q to W

5 V (score 1 point).
Giving each letter a value according to its position in the
alphabet, each word must have a total letter-value of 45.

The three letters of the unfinished word have a total of 23, which must be increased to 45 with the addition of 22 — that is, the 22nd letter of the alphabet — *V*.

6   b **(score 1 point)**.

7   66 **(score 1 point)**.

The numbers at the top are divisible by 3 and 4 alternately.

The only number in the bottom line that is divisible by 3 is *66*.

8   **(Score 1 point if all correct; $\frac{1}{2}$ point if 7 correct)**.

The disposition of the letters from A to H indicates that the words are considered in a clockwise direction. Starting with PAPER, and reading clockwise:

    paper
(A) MONEY
    spider
(B) CRAB
    apple
(C) JACK
    pot
(D) SHOT
    gun
(E) DOG
    collar
(F) BONE
    dry
(G) CLEAN
    cut
(H) GLASS
    paper

9   (D) **(score 1 point)**.

Apart from KIWI, which is a non-flying bird and also a

slang term for a non-flying member of the New Zealand Air Force, the others are all acronyms (words formed from the initial letters of other words):

(A) ANZAC Australian and New Zealand Army Corps;
(B) NATO North Atlantic Treaty Organization;
(C) PLUTO Pipe line under the ocean;
(E) NAAFI Navy, Army and Air Force Institute.

10 A 32; B 38 (score 1 point if both correct; ½ point if 1 correct).

	A	B
1st move	18	20
	3	5
	9	11
2nd move	25	19
	4	6
	16	10
3rd move	24	18
	5	7
	15	9
4th move	23	25
	6	8
	14	16
5th move	22	24
	7	1
	13	15
6th move	21	23
	8	2
	12	14
7th move	20	22
	1	3
	11	13
Total	32	38

11 6 (score 1 point).

Correcting the spacing, the series becomes:
1 8 27 64 125 21–

That is: the cubes of: 1, 2, 3, 4, 5, 6. The cube of 6 is 216, which means that *6* must follow 21.

12 R (score 1 point).

Substituting numbers for letters according to their position in the alphabet, each horizontal row adds to 20.

Therefore, X must be 18, as it is paired with 2, and R is the 18th letter.

13 A 5; B 2; C 12 (score 1 point if all correct; ½ point if 2 correct).

Consider the movements of the black section in each figure. It goes diagonally across the square from bottom left to top right and then back again:

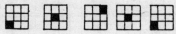

In the circle it moves two segments at a time in a clockwise direction:

In the diamond it moves alternately from top to bottom:

14 22 (score 1 point).

In each quarter of the circle:
add the numbers in the outer ring; subtract the sum of the numbers in the next ring; add the sum of the numbers in the

next ring to give the number that goes into the inner
section.

Thus:

the sum of 2, 3, 4 and 5 14

subtract the sum of 1, 2, 3 and 4 10

4

add the sum of 3, 4, 5 and 6 18

22

15 C **(score 1 point).**

The relative positions are shown below:

	1	2	3	4	5	6	7	8	9	10	11	12	13	14	15	16	17	18	19	20	21	22	23	24	25
A	1		2			3				4					5						6				
B		1			2			3				4						5							
C			1				2				3						4								5

Remember to keep a note of your score.

NOTES

Questions 4, 7, 8, 10 and 13 probably gave most difficulty.
Regarding 4, and as you may meet other problems of this
nature, it is worth bearing in mind the coincidence that there
are 52 cards in a pack — or 26 in half a pack (the equivalent
of two suits) — and 26 letters in the alphabet. Your friendly

inquisitor, having stumbled on this fact, may well feel at liberty to use the tactic again in the future!

I was amused to witness the antics of some volunteers who were trying to fathom the answer to No 6. Holding the page upside-down, and even holding it up to the light and trying to see through it from the reverse side were common ploys.

As to No 11, you were advised previously to keep an eye open for series — such as this — which were incorrectly spaced. My hope is that you benefited from past experience.

TEST 2
(Time limit: 1 hour)
(You may rest after 30 minutes and
then resume for a further 30 minutes)

1 Which of the numbered arrows belongs to x?

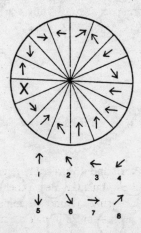

2   What goes into the last rectangle?

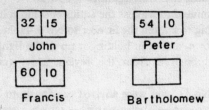

32	15
John

54	10
Peter

60	10
Francis

Bartholomew

3   Pinion A is the driving pinion, while pinion B idles on its stub axle.

The black teeth of these pinions are in mesh with teeth in the outer ring.

(A) After four revolutions of A in an anti-clockwise direction, where will the black tooth of pinion B be?

(B)   And where will it be when A has revolved clockwise through one revolution and then to where the tooth marked x meshes with the outer ring?

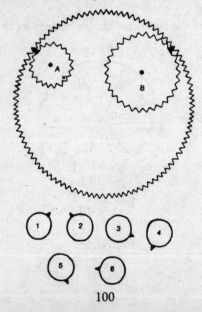

4 Which of the numbers in the bottom line should be placed under 17 in the top line?

 2 3   4 5   6 7 8 10 11 17
 7 2 17 6 13 8 3   5   4

 9 15 20 33 21 25

5 What comes next in this series?
      I S I T P N A A
      D L I I Y N –

6 Supply words which will go into the brackets. Each word must link logically with the preceding word and the following word, e.g. tea (POT) roast.

CUPBOARD
(   )
LETTER
(   )
STRONG
(   )
KITE
(   )
TIME
(   )
SHELL
(   )
WAVE
(   )
WISE
(   )
POT

7 Imagine that blocks x and y are removed from the arrangement below, and that the remaining shape is turned upside-down.

Which of the other shapes will result?

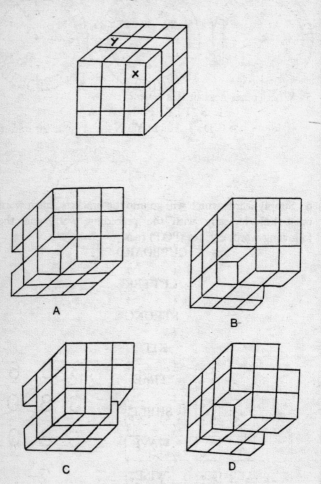

102

8 These clocks are all wrong, as indicated. If they are all correctly adjusted, which clock will show the nearest time to 12 o'clock?

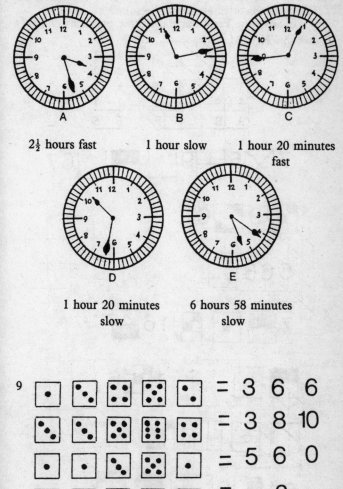

A

B

C

$2\frac{1}{2}$ hours fast

1 hour slow

1 hour 20 minutes fast

D

E

1 hour 20 minutes slow

6 hours 58 minutes slow

9

= 3 6 6

= 3 8 10

= 5 6 0

= ?

10 What comes next?

```
2 3 4 6 1 2 2 0
1 8 4 8 1 0 -
```

11 Discover the key from these three problems and then break this NAVAL code.

```
                           2  1
         1  2              2  2
         3  4      6  8    1  3
         4  9      5  2    1  1
         ─────    ─────   ─────
         A  B      T  E    E  S
```

12 Which is the odd one out?
   (A) OUTSTRIP
   (B) RED CURRANT
   (C) SIGHING
   (D) SELF-EDUCATED
   (E) BIG FEET
   (F) IRON-MOULD

13 Without using a pocket calculator, which of these investments would give the greatest interest?
   (A) £1,000 @ 5% simple interest for 4 years;
   (B) £700 @ 8% compound interest for 3 years;
   (C) £900 @ 7% simple interest for 3 years;
   (D) £800 @ 6% compound interest for 4 years.

14 Give values for A, B and C:

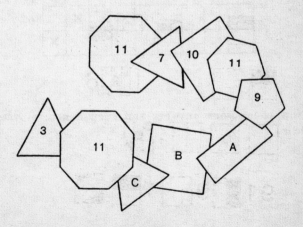

15 Write words for which the definitions are given:
1 No lover of foreigners.
2 Remove objectionable reading-matter.
3 Stuffing art!
4 Still valid.
5 Not liable for duty.
6 Joint.
7 Headwear — for holding medicinal preparations?
8 Correct on religious doctrine.
9 It receives the post.

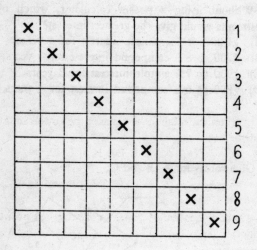

Now check your answers and keep a note of your score.

ANSWERS

1 4 (score 1 point).

Start with the arrow above X. In the opposite segment it is turned 90 degrees anti-clockwise. The next is turned 90 degrees clockwise. This alternating rotation is continued. Therefore, in the opposite segment to X the arrow must be turned 90 degrees clockwise (No 4).

2 (Score 1 point if correct).

Add the letter-values of the consonants according to their position in the alphabet and enter the total in the left-hand side.

Then enter the total of the value of the vowels in the right-hand side:

B 2; R 18; T 20; H 8; L 12;

M 13; W 23 .... Total 96

A 1; O 15; O 15; E 5 ....Total 36

3 (Score 1 point if both correct; ½ point if 1 correct).

(A) 5; (B) 1

There are 20 teeth on A and 30 on B.

The large annular ring will rotate in the same direction as the driving pinion.

(A) After 4 revolutions of A the outer ring will rotate anti-clockwise through 80 teeth, causing the idling pinion to rotate through 2 revolutions (60 teeth) and an additional 20 teeth.

(B) The driving pinion will rotate through 30 teeth — the same number as on the idling pinion, which will bring the black tooth on B to where it was originally (1).

4 20 (score 1 point).

Even numbers have prime numbers beneath them. Prime numbers have even numbers beneath them. 17 is a prime number, and must have an even number beneath it.

The only even number in the third line is *20*.

5 A (score 1 point).

There are three separate series. Starting with the first letter and taking every third letter thereafter:

   I T A L Y

Starting with the second letter and taking every third letter thereafter:

   S P A I N

From the third letter:

   I N D I *A*

6 (score 1 point if all correct; $\frac{1}{2}$ if 6 or 7 correct).

cupboard
LOVE
letter
HEAD
strong
BOX
kite
MARK
time
BOMB
shell
SHOCK
wave
LENGTH
wise
CRACK
pot

7 **B (score 1 point).**

Removing blocks x and y leaves the following:

Turned upside-down, this corresponds with *B*.

8 **D (score 1 point).**

When adjusted, the clocks show the following times:

A	from	3.27 to 12.57
B	from	11.13 to 12.13
C	from	1.44 to 12.24
D	from	10.32 to 11.52
E	from	5.21 to 12.19

9 **2 4 12 (score 1 point if all correct; ½ point if 2 correct).**

The first number equals the number of CENTRE spots.

The second number is the total of the spots that surround the centre spots.

The third number is the total of the remaining spots.

10 **0 (score 1 point).**

There are three separate series, though digits representing tens are not placed adjacent to the units. For example, 12 is shown as 1 2. Starting with the first term, each third term thereafter multiplies the previous term by 3:

   2 – – 6 – – – – 18 – – – – –

Starting with the second term, each third term thereafter multiplies the previous term by 4:

$- 3 - - 12 - - - - 48 - - -$

Starting with the third term, each third term thereafter multiplies the previous term by 5:

$- - 4 - - - 20 - - - - 100.$

The final term (to complete 100) is *0*.

11 SUBMARINES HAVE BEEN SIGHTED IN THE NORTH ATLANTIC (score 1 point).

From the sum on the right it is obvious that S is 7. It must be decided whether the middle one is an addition or a subtraction, but it cannot be an addition, because it would then have a three digit answer. As it must be a subtraction, E must be 6 and T must be 1.

The left-hand problem must be an addition, so B must be 5 and A must be 9.

Substituting these letters in the code:

```
S - B - A - - - E S
- A - E
B E E -
S - - - T E -
- -   T - E
- - - T -
A T - A - T - -
```

Certain possible words now become apparent, such as SUBMARINES and ATLANTIC.

The third word (4 letters) and the sixth word (3 letters) are worth considering:

```
B E E -   T - E
```

The first must be BEER or BEEN, and the second must be THE, TIE or TOE. As it is unlikely that the seventh word ends in TI or TO, but could probably end in TH, it is reasonable to assume that the sixth word is THE. By substituting H wherever it occurs:

```
S - B - A - - N E S   H A - E   B E E N
S - - H T E -   - N   T H E   N - - T H
            A T - A N T - -
```

110

Even if by now the other words do not become apparent, the last word should be obvious:

A T - A N T - -

(remembering that it is a *naval* code).

This will supply L, I and C, and the rest should fall into place.

12 (C) (score 1 point).

SIGHING contains three letters in alphabetical order — GHI.

All the others contain three letters in *reverse* alphabetical order:

(A) oUTStrip
(B) rED-Currant
(D) selF-EDucated
(E) biG FEet
(F) irON-Mould

13 (D) (score 1 point).

(A) would show £200 interest;
(B) would show £182 interest;
(C) would show £189 interest;
(D) would show £210 interest.

14 A is 8; B is 7; C is 11 (score 1 point if all correct).

Starting at the octagon (11) at top left and moving clockwise, add the number of sides to the figure to the number of sides on its adjacent figure.

The figure before A is a pentagon (5 sides) and has a value of 9 (5 added to A, which is a square). Therefore, A (4 sides) is added to B (also 4 sides), giving A a value of 8.

B (4 sides) is added to C (a triangle), giving B a value of 7.

C (3 sides) is added to the next figure (an octagon), giving C a value of 11.

15 (Score 1 point if all correct; $\frac{1}{2}$ point if 7 or 8 correct).

1 X E N O P H O B E
2 E X P U R G A T E
3 T A X I D E R M Y
4 U N E X P I R E D
5 U N T A X A B L E
6 C O N N E X I O N
7 P I L L B O X E S
8 O R T H O D O X Y
9 L E T T E R B O X

Remember to keep a note of your score.

NOTES

No 5 was another example of a 'multiple' series, in which every third factor was taken, instead of every consecutive one. Your previous experience of this type of series may have stood you in good stead.

Several points may have been lost in No 6, particularly with KITE MARK. This is the symbol of the British Standards Institute. BOX KITE may also have caught you out.

A great deal of time *had* to be spent on Nos 8, 11 and 13. 13, of course, could have been solved much faster with the aid of a pocket calculator. Incidentally, the yields given in the answer ignore decimal fractions.

Hardly anybody succeeded with No 9 — hardly surprising, as there was little beyond sheer inspiration to guide you on your way.

In case I am accused — in No 11 — of not giving a totally

unambiguous solution to *every* coded letter, I can only claim that, as it was a *naval* code, S – B – A – – N E S and A T – A N T – – could reasonably be assumed to lead to SUBMARINES and ATLANTIC. The seventh word (NORTH), though with only – – – T H to go on, could not have been south, as S had already been accounted for. Finally, H A – E (following a plural word) could be taken as HAVE.

TEST 3
(Time limit: 45 minutes)

1 What goes into the brackets?

$$31 \quad (68216) \quad 48$$
$$19 \quad (28184) \quad 42$$
$$36 \quad (\qquad) \quad 47$$

2 Can you make anything of this?

3 What goes into the vacant square?

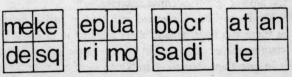

4 Which piece completes the jigsaw puzzle?

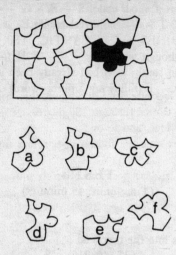

5 What comes next?

$1\frac{2}{3}$ $2 \cdot 75$ $3 \cdot 8$ $4\frac{5}{6}$

$5\frac{6}{7}$ $6 \cdot 875$ –

6 What letter should fill the empty space?

7 In four years' time I shall be five times as old as I was sixteen years ago. How old am I?

8   Which letter is in the wrong line?
          AHIMOSTUVWXY
          BCDEFGJKLNPQRZ

9   All these vanes move 90 degrees at a time. The longer ones rotate clockwise, first one move, then missing one and moving two (that is, through 180 degrees), then missing two and moving three, and so on.

At the same time the shorter ones rotate anti-clockwise in the same way.

What will be their positions after six moves?

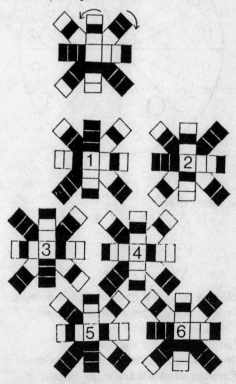

10 The black ball moves one position at a time clockwise.

If it stops on an even number the white ball moves one position clockwise.

If it stops on an odd number the white ball moves two positions anti-clockwise.

On what number will both balls be in the same position?

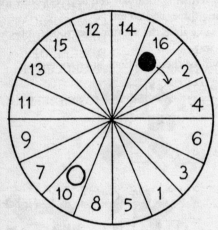

11 What comes next?

    13 122 83 314 305 3 163

12 A colour is concealed in each of these sentences:

  (A) Temper or anger are signs of weakness.
  (B) The money is for Edward.
  (C) You'll find I got it elsewhere.
  (D) One dancer, I see, is out of step.
  (E) 'I'm a gent and a lady's man,' he said.

13 Find a word that fits the first definition and then, by changing one letter only, a word that fits the second definition.

(A)	RADIO	–	INDEFATIGABLE
(B)	TRAIN	–	REMAINDER
(C)	PERSON HELD AS PLEDGE	–	PAYMENT FOR MAIL
(D)	PENITENT	–	DEVISE
(E)	RECOIL	–	MOTION OF WAVE
(F)	KNEAD	–	COMMUNICATION
(G)	WEDLOCK	–	DEPORTMENT
(H)	MODIFY STATEMENT	–	DEGREE OF EXCELLENCE
(I)	NAVAL VESSEL	–	IDOLIZE
(J)	YIELD	–	MOST DIFFICULT

14 Here are six clocks turned upside-down. *Without turning the page,* which shows the nearest time to 2.25 if held in front of a mirror?

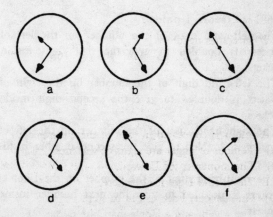

15 Complete the last line:

$$17 \quad (35) \quad 19$$
$$22 \quad (46) \quad 26$$
$$31 \quad (65) \quad 37$$
$$44 \quad (92) \quad 52$$
$$- \quad (-) \quad -$$

Now check your answers and keep a note of your score.

ANSWERS

1   681214 **(score 1 point).**

The left-hand digit of the number on the left of the brackets is doubled to give the first digit inside the brackets.

The left-hand digit of the number on the right of the brackets is doubled to give the second digit inside the brackets.

The right-hand digit of the number on the left of the brackets is doubled to give the second number inside the brackets.

The right-hand digit of the number on the right of the brackets is doubled to give the next number inside the brackets.

2 THIS (score 1 point).

Move the top pieces to the left and down.
Move the bottom pieces to the right and up.

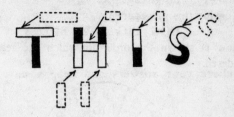

3 ke (score 1 point).

From the top left quarter in the first square, move one position anti-clockwise throughout:

me ri di an

Use the same procedure in the other quarters:

de mo cr at
sq ua bb le
ke ep sa *ke*

4 B (score 1 point).

5 (Score 1 point).

Express all the terms as vulgar fractions:

$$1\tfrac{2}{3} \quad 2\tfrac{3}{4} \quad 3\tfrac{4}{5} \quad 4\tfrac{5}{6} \quad 5\tfrac{6}{7} \quad 6\tfrac{7}{8}$$

Now it is obvious that the terms progress like this:

123 234 345 456 567 678 –

and that the final term must be 789, expressed as a vulgar fraction as in the examples:

$$7\tfrac{8}{9}$$

6 L (score 1 point).

Starting from C, read the opposite letter (A) and then return to the opposite side, moving clockwise to the next position (T). This gives CAT.

Following this procedure:

DOG PIG SOW BUL(*L*)

Below is shown the order in which the segments are considered:

7 21 (score 1 point).

If x represents my present age, then x + 4 = 5(x − 16).

Therefore: x + 4 = 5x − 80, from which: 84 = 4x, so x = 21.

8 S (score 1 point).

All the letters in the top line *except* S will read the same if reflected in a mirror.

S should be in the bottom line, in which every letter would read backwards if reflected in a mirror.

9 5 (score 1 point).

10   15 (score 1 point).

The balls move as follows:

Black ball	White ball
2	7
4	9
6	11
3	7
1	8
5	1
8	5
10	8
7	1
9	6
11	2
13	14
15	*15*

11   0 (score 1 point).

Correctly spaced, the series becomes:

> 1   31   2   28   3   31   4   30   5   31   6   3–

The series is based on the days and months of the year — the month followed by the number of days. June has 30 days, so the final term should be *30*.

12   (Score 1 point if all correct).

  (A)   ORANGE
  (B)   RED
  (C)   INDIGO
  (D)   CERISE
  (E)   MAGENTA

13 **(Score 1 point if all correct; ½ point if 8 or 9 correct).**

   (A) WIRELESS — TIRELESS
   (B) RETINUE — RESIDUE
   (C) HOSTAGE — POSTAGE
   (D) CONTRITE — CONTRIVE
   (E) BACKLASH — BACKWASH
   (F) MASSAGE — MESSAGE
   (G) MARRIAGE — CARRIAGE
   (H) QUALIFY — QUALITY
   (I) WARSHIP — WORSHIP
   (J) HARVEST — HARDEST

14 d **(score 1 point).**

15 61 (127) 71 **(score 1 point).**

The numbers on each side of the brackets alternately increase by 2, 3, 4, 5, 6, 7, 8 (and hence 9 and 10). To discover the number inside the brackets: double the number on the left and add 1, then 2, then 3, then 4, and finally 5 (122 plus 5 — *127*).

Remember to keep a note of your score.

Now total all your scores for the three tests in this section and check your rating from the following section, after which you can find your complete rating for all the tests.

NOTES

Greatest difficulty was experienced by the volunteers with 3, 6, 9 and 11, though, in the case of 11, you were warned to look out for series which are incorrectly spaced. When this was realised, and the series spaced correctly, the relationship between months and days should have become apparent.

The salient clue to solving No 3 was the fact that q is always followed by u. This leads to the fact that SQ in square 1 must be followed by UA in the next square. This combination may have pointed to the order in which *all* the letters were positioned.

In the answers I offered an algebraic solution to No 7, though it could be (and probably was) solved by trial and error. Unless making lucky choices in the latter case, algebra offered the quickest solution.

The most time-consuming problems were 3, 9, 13 and (in particular) 10.

RATINGS IN GROUP III

TEST 1 ..... Average $4\frac{1}{2}$ points
TEST 2 ..... Average 5 points
TEST 3 ..... Average $5\frac{1}{2}$ points

Total for the Group

Out of a possible 45 points:

Over 30	..... Excellent
22 – 29	..... Very good
16 – 21	..... Good
15	..... Average
10 – 14	..... Fair
Under 10	..... Poor

Although the average score was very low, it must be acknowledged that many of the problems in this group were very difficult indeed. However, lest it should be thought that they were *too* difficult, a few problems which completely baffled the majority were solved with relative ease by others — once again proving the point that aptitude has a major influence on the results. Those who fared well in the numerical tests may have done badly on the verbal tests, and so on.

Now find your overall total score for all the tests, and then find your rating from the next page.

OVERALL RATINGS FOR
ALL THE TESTS

The total number of possible points is 165.

The average score throughout was:

GROUP I 35
GROUP II 26
GROUP III 15
TOTAL: 76

Over 130	....	Excellent
108 – 129	....	Very good
77 – 107	....	Good
76	....	Average
60 – 75	....	Fair
Under 60	....	Poor

Although, as clearly stated at the beginning of this book, it makes no claim to quantify your 'intelligence' in terms of an 'IQ', the results indicate that 76 is the norm, which could be taken to represent an IQ of 100.

Certainly, anything over 130 indicates a *very* high IQ, while a range between 100 and 129 implies a high IQ and one that is above 100.

I am afraid 70 or under indicates a low IQ — in so far as psychometric tests of this nature can have any credibility.

But take heart! Such tests only cover a limited number of subjects — mainly of an academic nature. It may well be that even if you had a very low score you are more adapted to tests requiring manual dexterity. A brilliant mathematician is not necessarily a good carpenter or gardener.